Boundless Minds

OrangeBooks Publication

1st Floor, Rajhans Arcade, Mall Road, Kohka, Bhilai, Chhattisgarh 490020

Website: **www.orangebooks.in**

© Copyright, 2024, Author

All rights reserved. No part of this book may be reproduced, stored in a retrieval system, or transmitted, in any form by any means, electronic, mechanical, magnetic, optical, chemical, manual, photocopying, recording or otherwise, without the prior written consent of its writer.

First Edition, 2024

BOUNDLESS MINDS

A Creative Canvas
for Imaginative Youth

MADHUR DUBEY & RAKESH DUBEY

OrangeBooks Publication
www.orangebooks.in

तेषां सततयुक्तानां भजतां प्रीतिपूर्वकम् ।

ददामि बुद्धियोगं तं येन मामुपयान्ति ते ॥

BG 10.10: To those whose minds are always united with Me in loving devotion, I give the divine knowledge by which they can attain Me.

UNLEASHING THE POWER OF IMAGINATION

In the symphony of gratitude, I extend my heartfelt thanks to my four children, the architects of inspiration in my life, marked by academic achievements that include three A's and a solitary M. Their accomplishments have served as a poignant reminder of the profound impact of shared learning between parent and child, shaping my perspective on the transformative power of education.

A pivotal moment transpired when my son Avirbhav and his brother Arnav challenged the traditional notions of education, asserting that the expanse of knowledge lay readily available through artificial intelligence on the internet. This paradigm shift prompted me to reevaluate my stance, leading me to the discovery of Chat GPT-a tool that effortlessly encapsulates what I term **"intellect"** in a single click.

The horizon of possibilities expanded further when I stumbled upon news about Elon Musk's venture into developing a chip for human brains, envisioning a future where educational intellect could be accessed with a mere click. However, I realized that while this intellect serves as a potent tool, its effective utilization hinges on the seed of intelligence-(**imagination**).

Fond memories from my school days resurfaced when my father encouraged me to pursue Tabla (Music) classes and gifted me a splendid flute. He, a steadfast pillar in my family, not only advocated for academic excellence but also nurtured my imagination. I often fondly refer to him as the "**Gyan**" I hold. Complementing his influence, my mother embodied devotion, **"Bhakti"** teaches me the virtues of humility and surrender to the divine-an essential foundation for nurturing new realms of imagination.

This book, a testament to my experiences, pays homage to the three goddesses in my life-RITU, MUKTI, and AARVEE.

Ritu, my wife, became my guide in the practice of yoga, unlocking the doors to imagination during meditative states. Mukti, my sister, assumed the role of a guru during a moment of crisis when her dress caught fire on Diwali. In that daunting situation, she imparted a profound lesson on imagining positivity amid adversity.

Aarvee, my angelic daughter, exemplifies a kaleidoscope of colors and expressions. When I queried the source of her imaginative ideas, she pointed to the sky, revealing clouds that metamorphosed into an elephant and a cart. Her uninhibited creativity became a testament to the boundless potential residing within us all.

Firmly rooted in the belief that we now possess the power of intellect, I advocate for its conscientious exercise to channel our collective energies towards positive imagination. It is through this transformative journey that we can create wonders beyond our wildest dreams.

Embarking on the fifteen-step journey of imagination, this book serves as a guid-a testament to the inherent potential within each of us. May the pages that follow inspire, provoke thought, and ignite the flames of creativity. Together, let us unravel the tapestry of imagination and usher in a future where innovation knows no bounds.

A profound note of gratitude extends to my circle of FRIEND'S, Anurag, Sandeep, Siddhartha, Mohan Sathe, Vivek, Gargey, Himalay, and the Bhopali gang, whose collective presence has played a pivotal role in shaping and refining my imagination skills. Through the tapestry of shared experiences, late Vikas Shukla's memory remains a cherished part of this journey-a testament to the enduring impact of friendship on the evolution of imagination. The vibrant tapestry of these friendships, especially during our travels, has served as a crucible for envisioning the seemingly impossible, inspiring Chapters 13 and 14 of this book.

→·※·←

Contents

- **Chapter 1**
  The Wonderful World Of Imagination 1

- **Chapter 2**
  The Enchanting Magic Of Creativity 5

- **Chapter 3**
  The Magical Power Of Stories 11

- **Chapter 4**
  The Wonderful World Of Imaginary Friends And Play 17

- **Chapter 5**
  Dreaming Big: Unleashing The Power Of Your Imagination 23

- **Chapter 6**
  The Art Of Imagination: Visualization Techniques 29

- ➢ **Chapter 7**

  The Enchanted Realms: Exploring Fantasy And Creating Worlds 35

- ➢ **Chapter 8**

  The Imagination Circus: A Spectacular Show Of Creativity 41

- ➢ **Chapter 9**

  Art And Expression: Unleashing The Imagination Canvas 49

- ➢ **Chapter 10**

  The Scientific Imagination: Discovering Wonders Through Curiosity 57

- ➢ **Chapter 11**

  The Mindful Imagination: Where Creativity Meets Presence 65

- ➢ **Chapter 12**

  The Problem-Solving Quest: Unleashing Imagination's Superpowers 73

- ➢ **Chapter 13**

  The Collaborative Imagination Carnival: A Celebration Of Shared Creativity 81

➢ **Chapter 14**

Imagination Across Borders..................................89

➢ **Chapter 15**

Reflection And Celebration Carnival 97

➤※◄

Chapter 1

The Wonderful World of Imagination

In the grand tapestry of human existence, the power of imagination has been celebrated since time immemorial. A testament to this lies in ancient myths and tales, where divine beings harnessed the extraordinary potential of imagination to shape worlds and weave realities. One such profound narrative is the story of Brahma, the Hindu creator deity, who, with the assistance of Saraswati, the goddess of knowledge and arts, brought the universe into being through the divine force of imagination.

Just as Brahma wove the cosmos with divine creativity, our young adventurers in the land of endless possibilities are about to embark on a journey that celebrates the wonders of imagination. This prelude sets the stage for the magical exploration of the incredible landscapes that reside within the fertile realms of young minds. Imagination, as both a divine and human gift, bridges worlds, ignites creativity, and propels dreams into reality. So, dear readers, as we step into "The Wonderful World of Imagination," let the echoes of ancient tales and the whispers of boundless creativity guide us through the enchanted corridors of imagination's majestic kingdom.

What is Imagination?

Imagine a world where you can soar through the clouds on the back of a rainbow-colored dragon, where talking animals share their wisdom, and where you can build a castle made of chocolate with just a thought. That, dear friends, is the enchanting realm of imagination!

Imagination is like a superpower that lets you create pictures in your mind, dream up fantastical adventures, and even turn your bedroom into a pirate ship sailing the seven seas. It's the ability to see things that others might not, like invisible friends or a tea party with teddy bears.

But it's not just about seeing - imagination is a treasure chest of ideas and stories. It's the secret ingredient that transforms a cardboard box into a spaceship or a simple stick into a magical wand. Imagination is your passport to worlds beyond the ordinary, where the extraordinary happens.

Why is Imagination Important?

Now, you might wonder, "Why should I bother with this thing called imagination?" Well, buckle up, because imagination is your ticket to a world of fun, learning, and endless possibilities!

1. **Creativity Unleashed:** Imagination and creativity go hand in hand, like peanut butter and jelly! When you let your imagination run wild, you become a master creator. Who knows? You might design the next amazing invention or paint a masterpiece that makes people say, "Wow!"
2. **Problem-Solving Superpower:** Imagine you're faced with a tricky puzzle or a challenging problem. What do you do? You call upon your imagination superhero! It helps you think outside the box, come up with clever solutions, and turn obstacles into exciting adventures.
3. **Dream Big, Achieve Big:** Imagination is like a compass guiding you toward your dreams. When you dream big and let your imagination lead the way, you open doors to a future filled with endless opportunities. From becoming an astronaut to a famous chef, your imagination is the first step to making those dreams come true.
4. **Friendship and Fun:** Imagination is the key to a world where anything is possible, and laughter is the universal language. It's what turns a simple playdate into a journey to a magical kingdom or a quest to find hidden treasures. Imagination makes every moment an adventure!

So, dear adventurers, get ready to embark on this thrilling quest into the heart of imagination! As we explore together, remember the words of the wise Dr. Seuss: **"Think left and think right, think low and think high. Oh, the thinks you can think if only you try!"** Let your imagination soar, and let the adventure begin!

Chapter 2

The Enchanting Magic of Creativity

Welcome, young dreamers, to a captivating journey into "The Enchanting Magic of Creativity." Before we embark on this exploration, let's draw inspiration from "The Story of Markandeya." In this ancient tale, Markandeya's encounter with Yama, the god of death, unveils the profound depths of devotion and the incredible resilience of the human mind.

Similarly, creativity possesses a mystical essence that transcends boundaries and limitations. Just as Markandeya's devotion defied the grip of time and death, creativity empowers you to surpass the ordinary, transforming your thoughts into timeless wonders.

"The Enchanting Magic of Creativity" invites you to enter a realm where imagination and creativity perform an intricate dance. Picture the canvas as Markandeya's devotion, waiting to be adorned with the vivid colors of your ideas. Like Markandeya facing challenges with unwavering faith, creativity is your tool to confront the blank page and transform it into a captivating spectacle.

As you delve into the delightful activities designed to encourage your creative spirit, remember the resilience of Markandeya's mind in the face of adversity. In the world of creativity, there are no limits-no wrong ideas. Every stroke, every word, and every whimsical idea contributes to the masterpiece of your imagination.

So, dear dreamers, let "The Story of Markandeya" echo in your creative endeavors. Embrace the enchanting magic of creativity, where the mind, like devotion, holds the power to transcend limitations. Your canvas is ready, and with every imaginative creation, you become the architect of wonders beyond the grasp of ordinary reality. Now, unfurl the sails of your creativity and set forth on a journey where every stroke and every thought becomes a testament to the timeless magic you hold within.

What is Creativity?

Picture a canvas waiting to be painted, a stage set for a grand performance, or a blank page yearning for a story. That's the playground of creativity! Creativity is the art of turning ordinary things into extraordinary masterpieces. It's the spark that transforms a simple idea into something magnificent and uniquely yours.

Have you ever built a tower out of blocks and thought, "What if it could touch the clouds?" That, my friends, is your creative spirit at play! Creativity is the superhero cape you wear when you're crafting, drawing, or even telling a funny story.

The Dance of Creativity and Imagination

Now, let's imagine creativity and imagination as the best dance partners ever. They twirl and spin together, creating a spectacular performance just for you. Imagination plants the seeds, and creativity helps them bloom into vibrant flowers of ideas.

Close your eyes and imagine a world filled with polka-dotted elephants, rainbow-colored ice cream mountains, and talking trees that tell the silliest jokes. That's your imagination painting a colorful picture. Now, open your eyes, grab your crayons, and bring that wacky world to life! That's creativity in action.

Creativity takes your wildest thoughts and turns them into real, tangible wonders. It's the reason we have awe-inspiring artworks, catchy songs, and stories that transport us to far-off lands. When you unleash your creativity, you become a co-author of the universe, adding your unique flair to the grand story of life.

Encouraging Kids to Embrace Their Creative Side

Now, let's talk about you - the budding artists, storytellers, and inventors of tomorrow. Here's the golden rule: There's no such thing as a "wrong" idea in the world of creativity. Every scribble, every word, every crazy idea is like a puzzle piece waiting to fit into the grand masterpiece of your imagination.

1. **Doodle Delight:** Grab your favorite crayons, markers, or even mud if you're feeling adventurous. Doodle, draw, and let your hand lead the way. Remember, a scribble today might be a masterpiece tomorrow!

2. **Storytelling Spectacle:** Create your own stories filled with talking animals, flying carpets, or a pizza that tells jokes. Let your imagination run wild, and watch as your stories take on a life of their own.

3. **Crafty Adventures:** Raid the recycling bin, gather some glue and glitter, and transform ordinary objects into extraordinary creations. Cardboard boxes become castles, and toilet paper rolls become mighty telescopes.

4. **Dream Board Galore:** Cut out pictures from magazines or draw your dreams on a large sheet of paper. Your dream board is a visual treasure map guiding you toward your goals. What do you want to explore, create, or become?

Remember the wise words of Albert Einstein: **"Imagination is more important than knowledge. For knowledge is limited, whereas imagination embraces the entire world."** So, dear young creators, let your imagination and creativity dance freely, and let the magic unfold. The world is your canvas, and you are the artist creating a masterpiece with every thought, every idea, and every giggle. Now, go forth and create wonders beyond your wildest dreams!

Chapter 3

---※---

The Magical Power of Stories

This chapter is an invitation to young minds, beckoning them to explore the enchanted realms stories unveil. To illuminate the significance of storytelling, we draw inspiration from Hindu philosophy's cosmic perspective- Lord Vishnu's Dreams, where the entire universe is considered a dream.

Much like Lord Vishnu's cosmic dream, stories unfold as vivid dreams in the theatre of our minds. They transport us to realms beyond reality, where dragons breathe life into the skies, fairies sprinkle magic, and knights embark on noble quests. The power of stories lies not just in their narratives but in the imaginative sparks they ignite.

In the following pages, as we delve into "The Magical Power of Stories," consider the parallels between the cosmic dream and the dreams spun by stories. Both underscore the imaginative nature of reality, inviting young adventurers to embrace the boundless possibilities that emerge when the door to imagination swings open. So, with the cosmic dreams as our guide, let us embark on this chapter and discover the transformative magic that stories hold within their enchanting pages.

The Magical Power of Stories

Once Upon a Time...

Close your eyes and imagine a world where dragons soar through the skies, fairies sprinkle magic dust, and brave knights embark on daring quests. Where are you? You're in the mesmerizing realm of stories! Stories are like magical carpets that whisk us away to places far beyond our wildest dreams.

What is the Power of Stories?

Stories have the power to paint vivid pictures in our minds, to make us laugh, cry, and feel a whole range of emotions. They are like windows into different worlds, allowing us to peek into the lives of characters who become our friends and mentors. Whether it's a bedtime story told by a loved one or a book that transports you to a far-off land, stories have a magic that is truly one-of-a-kind.

Imagine you're a pirate sailing the high seas, searching for hidden treasure. Or perhaps you're a space explorer zooming through galaxies unknown. Stories take you on these incredible journeys, unlocking the door to endless possibilities and igniting the flames of your imagination.

The Role of Imagination in Storytelling

Now, let's unveil the secret behind these magical tales - it's the extraordinary power of imagination! Every story begins with a sprinkle of imagination, transforming words on a page into a gateway to fantastical worlds.

1. **Character Creations:** Close your eyes and imagine a character, any character. It could be a friendly monster, a mischievous fairy, or a talking animal. Now, think about their adventures, their challenges, and the lessons they learn. Congratulations, you've just created a story in your mind!

2. **Setting Spectacles:** Picture a place where anything is possible - a candy forest, a cloud city, or an underwater kingdom. The setting of a story is like the stage where your imagination sets the scene. You can create worlds more magical than you ever thought possible.

3. **Plot Perfections:** Every great story has a plot, a series of events that keep us turning the pages. What if a superhero lost their powers or a wizard discovered a hidden realm? Your imagination weaves the plot, creating twists and turns that keep the adventure alive.

4. **Lesson Lands:** Stories often carry messages and lessons. Imagine a tale where kindness defeats the

grumpiest of dragons or where teamwork saves the day. Your imagination is the guiding light that helps convey important messages through the power of storytelling.

😊 Jokes and Quotes Corner 😊

"The more that you read,

the more things you will know.

The more that you learn,

the more places you'll go."

- Dr. Seuss

Now, let's sprinkle in a bit of humor. **Why did the book go to therapy? Because it had too many issues!** *Laughter is the magic potion that makes stories even more delightful. So, here's a challenge: come up with your own silly, imaginative joke and share it with your friends.*

Embarking on Your Own Story Adventure

Now, dear readers, it's your turn to become storytellers and explorers of your imagination. Grab a pen, some paper, or even a magical quill, and let your imagination run wild. Create characters, build worlds, and let the stories flow from your heart. Remember, the power of stories is in your hands, and the magic of imagination is your guide. As J.K. Rowling once said, **"We do not**

need magic to transform our world. We carry all the power we need inside ourselves already. We have the power to imagine better." So, imagine away, and let the adventures begin!

Chapter 4

The Wonderful World of Imaginary Friends and Play

In the cosmic ballet of existence, the dance of imagination and play finds resonance in ancient myths, echoing the rhythmic pulse that underlies creation. Among these, Lord Shiva's Tandava Dance stands as a symbol of the universe's rhythmic and creative nature, illustrating the profound connection between movement and imagination.

As we step into "The Wonderful World of Imaginary Friends and Play," consider the parallel between the cosmic dance of Lord Shiva and the lively dance of imagination in the hearts of young dreamweavers. Both showcase the transformative power of movement, rhythm, and creative energy.

Just as Shiva's Tandava Dance weaves the fabric of the cosmos, this chapter invites young minds to partake in the cosmic dance of their imaginations. Imaginary friends become playful partners in this dance, pirouetting through tea parties, sharing joyful conversations, and collaborating in the creation of fantastical worlds. Imagination, like Lord Shiva's dance, is a celebration of the boundless creative potential inherent in the rhythmic flow of existence.

So, dear young dreamweavers, as we embark on this chapter, envision yourselves as participants in the cosmic dance of imagination and play. Let the magic unfold, and may the rhythm of creativity guide you through the enchanting realms of your own unique Tandava Dance.

Understanding the Concept of Imaginary Friends

Imagine a friend who's invisible, always ready for adventures, and has the most fantastic stories to share. That, my young companions, is the enchanting world of imaginary friends! These special pals exist in the realm of your imagination, waiting to join you on incredible journeys.

1. **Invisible Companions:** Close your eyes and imagine your very own imaginary friend. What do they look like? Do they have wings, wear funny hats, or have a tail that wiggles with excitement? Imaginary friends are your personal companions, created by the magic of your imagination.

2. **Tea Parties and Treehouse Tales:** Imaginary friends love tea parties with cookies that never run out and treehouses where secrets are shared. They're

the perfect playmates for make-believe adventures, helping you explore uncharted territories and discover hidden treasures in your imagination.

3. **Joyful Conversations:** Have you ever chatted with your imaginary friend about your day or shared your dreams with them? Imaginary friends are wonderful listeners, always ready to lend an ear and sprinkle a bit of magic into your thoughts.

4. **Creative Collaborators:** Imaginary friends are like the coolest collaborators in your creativity team. They might inspire you to draw funny doodles, write silly songs, or even build forts that reach the clouds. With them by your side, every day becomes a canvas for imaginative masterpieces.

The Role of Imaginative Play in Development

Now, let's talk about a magical place called imaginative play - the superhighway to growing up with a heart full of joy and a mind brimming with creativity.

1. **Learning through Play:** When you engage in imaginative play, you're not just having fun; you're learning valuable life skills. Whether you're pretending to be a chef in a bustling kitchen or a space explorer discovering new planets, you're developing problem-solving, communication, and social skills.

2. **Building Empathy:** Playing with imaginary friends or stepping into different roles helps you understand others' feelings and perspectives. It's like wearing empathy glasses that allow you to see the world through someone else's eyes.

3. **Creativity Unleashed:** Imaginative play is the playground where your creativity gets to stretch its legs and run wild. It's the birthplace of superheroes, the setting for epic adventures, and the stage for stories that unfold in the most unexpected ways.

4. **Friendship Flourishes:** Through imaginative play, you create bonds with others that are as strong as a dragon's scales. Whether it's building a spaceship with your pals or hosting a teddy bear picnic, these shared adventures strengthen the magical thread that connects friends.

😊 Jokes and Quotes Corner 😊

"Logic will get you from A to B.

Imagination will take you everywhere."

- Albert Einstein

Now, let's sprinkle some laughter into our playtime. ***Why did the teddy bear say no to dessert? Because it was already stuffed!*** *Laughter and play go hand in hand, so don't forget to giggle your way through your imaginative escapades.*

Embracing the Magic Within

Dear imaginative souls, as you venture into the realms of imaginary friends and play, remember the wise words of C.S. Lewis**: "You are never too old to set another goal or to dream a new dream."** Let your imagination be your guide, and let the magic of play be the wind beneath your wings. So, gather your imaginary friends, leap into the world of play, and let the adventures unfold like the pages of a storybook. The magic is within you; now, go and play!

Chapter 5

Dreaming Big: Unleashing the Power of Your Imagination

The birth of Kartikeya, born out of the collective energy of the Devas, stands as a symbol of focused imagination and divine intention. As we delve into the chapter on dreaming big, the parallel emerges between the celestial birth of Kartikeya and the power that lies within the focused imagination of young dreamers.

Kartikeya's creation echoes the notion that when collective energies align with a common purpose, incredible feats can be achieved. This cosmic tale becomes an inspiring backdrop for the journey young visionaries are about to embark upon-a journey through the expansive landscapes of their own imagination.

Much like Kartikeya's birth shaped by divine intention, this chapter encourages young dreamers to harness the limitless power of imagination. The magical wand they possess, akin to the collective energy of the Devas, can transform their wildest dreams into a tangible reality. The adventure of dreaming big is an exploration of divine potential within, a journey guided by imagination, fueled by ambition, and illuminated by the belief that every dream is possible. As Kartikeya, with his celestial birth, became a beacon of divine potential, so too can young dreamers pave their way to extraordinary destinations through the magical power of dreaming big.

What Does It Mean to Dream Big?

Imagine you have a magical wand that can turn your wildest dreams into reality. That's the spirit of dreaming big! Dreaming big means imagining a future that goes beyond the ordinary, a future where you become the hero of your own story.

1. **The Power of Imagination:** Close your eyes and let your mind wander. Picture a world where you're soaring through the skies on the wings of a dragon or exploring the depths of the ocean as a fearless explorer. That, dear dreamers, is the playground of your imagination.

2. **Setting Goals:** Now, let's add a touch of reality to our dreams. Goals are like stepping stones that bridge the gap between imagination and achievement. Whether it's learning to play an instrument, becoming an astronaut, or creating a

robot friend, setting goals is the roadmap to turning dreams into reality.

3. **Imagination and Ambition:** Dreaming big is not just about wishing upon a star; it's about fueling your ambitions with the limitless power of imagination. The bigger you dream, the more room you create for growth, learning, and becoming the person you envision.

4. **Believe in the Impossible:** As Audrey Hepburn once said, **"Nothing is impossible; the word itself says 'I'm possible'!"** Dreaming big means believing in the potential within you, acknowledging that the impossible is merely a challenge waiting to be conquered.

The Adventure of Dreaming Big

Now, let's embark on a journey where your dreams are the compass guiding you to extraordinary destinations.

1. **Imagine Your Ideal Future:** Picture yourself in the future. What do you see? Are you a scientist discovering new planets, a chef creating magical recipes, or an artist painting the world with vibrant colors? Your imagination is the canvas; paint the future you desire.

2. **Create a Dream Board:** Gather magazines, scissors, and a big sheet of paper. Cut out pictures that represent your dreams and glue them onto your dream board. Hang it up where you can see it every

day - a visual reminder of the exciting adventures awaiting you.

3. **Meet Your Future Self:** Imagine meeting your future self. What advice would they give you? What accomplishments would they share? Let your imagination guide this meeting and inspire you to take steps today that your future self will thank you for.

4. **Share Your Dreams:** Don't keep your dreams locked away. Share them with friends, family, or even your imaginary friends! Talking about your dreams makes them feel real and sets the stage for the support and encouragement you'll need along the way.

😊 Jokes and Quotes Corner 😊

"The future belongs to those who believe in the beauty of their dreams."

- Eleanor Roosevelt.

Now, let's sprinkle some laughter into our dreams. ***Why did the pencil dream of becoming a paintbrush? Because it wanted to draw bigger dreams!*** *Laughter adds a touch of joy to our journey, so don't forget to share a smile with your fellow dreamers.*

Dream Big, Act Big

Dear dreamers, as you embark on the adventure of dreaming big, remember the wise words of Walt Disney: "If you can dream it, you can do it. **"Your imagination** is the compass, your goals are the map, and the journey is yours to explore. Dream big, aim high, and let the magic of your imagination pave the way to a future filled with endless possibilities."** The world is waiting for your dreams to unfold - now, go and make them a reality!

Chapter 6

The Art of Imagination: Visualization Techniques

In the timeless epic of the Ramayana, a captivating tale unfolds, revealing the deceptive power of imagination through the creation of the Golden Deer by Maricha. This illusion, designed to allure and deceive, mirrors the dual nature of imagination explored in the upcoming chapter on visualization. While imagination can be a tool of enchantment and creativity, it also possesses the ability to craft illusions that may lead one astray.

As we delve into "The Art of Imagination: Visualization Techniques," the parallel with the Golden Deer story emerges-a reminder that imagination, like a double-edged sword, can be both a creator of mesmerizing mental images and a harbinger of illusions. This chapter invites young visionaries to wield their imaginative powers consciously, steering them toward constructive visualization.

Much like the cautionary tale within the Ramayana, the exercises and techniques in this chapter aim to empower young minds to harness visualization for positive and transformative purposes. As they embark on the magical journey of mental imagery, the lessons from the Golden Deer story serve as a reminder to be mindful of the illusions that imagination can weave, encouraging them to navigate the landscape of their minds with wisdom and intention.

What is Visualization?

Imagine you have a magical movie screen in your mind where you can play scenes from your favorite adventures or create entirely new worlds. That's the enchanting essence of visualization! Visualization is the art of forming mental images, allowing you to see with your mind's eye and bring your ideas to life.

1. **Mind Movies:** Close your eyes and imagine a movie playing inside your head. What's happening? Are you soaring with dragons, dancing with fairies, or solving mysteries in a hidden jungle? Your mind is the director, and visualization is the ticket to your very own blockbuster.

2. **Creating Mental Images:** Visualization isn't just about seeing; it's about feeling, hearing, and experiencing with all your senses. Picture the smell of freshly baked cookies, the sound of ocean waves, or the sensation of floating in a cloud. Your mind is a canvas; let your senses paint the masterpiece.

3. **Turning Thoughts into Pictures:** Have you ever had an idea that felt like a light bulb flickering above your head? Visualization turns those flickers into

vibrant images. It's like turning the pages of a storybook, each image revealing a new chapter of your imagination.

Exercises to Unlock Your Visualization Powers

Now, let's embark on some fun and magical exercises that will turn your imagination into a kaleidoscope of colors and ideas.

1. **Imaginary Ice Cream Stand:**
    - Close your eyes and imagine you're at an ice cream stand.
    - Picture the colors, the flavors, and the toppings.
    - Can you smell the sweetness in the air?
2. **Magical Forest Adventure:**
    - Envision yourself in a magical forest.
    - What creatures do you encounter? Are there talking trees or mischievous fairies?
    - Feel the soft moss beneath your feet.
3. **Dream Vacation Postcard:**
    - Imagine you're on your dream vacation.
    - Picture the sun, the sand, or the snow.
    - Can you hear the laughter and feel the warmth?
4. **Invention Workshop:**
    - Pretend you have a workshop filled with gadgets and gizmos.

- Picture yourself inventing something amazing.
- What does it do, and how does it work?

Visualization for Problem-Solving

Visualization isn't just about creating pretty pictures; it's a superhero tool for solving problems and overcoming challenges.

1. The Puzzle Palace:
- Imagine you're in a palace filled with puzzles.
- See the pieces coming together in your mind.
- Can you visualize the solution before putting it into action?

2. Creative Blueprint:
- Before starting a project, visualize the end result.
- Picture the details and how it will feel when it's complete.
- Your imagination is the blueprint for success.

3. Future Explorer:
- Close your eyes and imagine your future self.
- What challenges did you overcome? What achievements are you celebrating?
- Use this mental image as motivation for solving today's problems.

4. Mindful Meditation:
- Practice mindfulness by visualizing a calming place.

- Picture yourself in a serene garden or floating on a cloud.
- Let the peaceful image guide you through problem-solving with a clear mind.

☺ Jokes and Quotes Corner ☺

"Logic will get you from A to B.

Imagination will take you everywhere."

- Albert Einstein.

Now, let's add a sprinkle of laughter. **Why did the tomato turn red? Because it saw the salad dressing!** *Laughter is the secret ingredient that makes your imagination shine even brighter.*

Closing Thoughts: Your Imagination's Best Friend

Dear young visionaries, as you explore the realms of visualization, remember the wise words of Roald Dahl: **"Those who don't believe in magic will never find it."** Your mind is a treasure trove of magic waiting to be discovered. Visualization is your passport to unlocking the wonders within. So, close your eyes, let your imagination dance, and watch as the world transforms into a canvas of endless possibilities. Your journey has just begun - now, visualize the extraordinary!

Chapter 7

The Enchanted Realms: Exploring Fantasy and Creating Worlds

The story of Narada Muni's cosmic travels stands as a testament to the imaginative and creative aspects of storytelling. As we embark on the chapter exploring the enchanting realms of fantasy, Narada Muni's journey becomes a metaphor for the boundless potential of the human imagination.

Much like Narada Muni, who traverses the universe, weaving tales that captivate the cosmos, young dreamweavers are invited to explore their own imaginative landscapes. The mythical wanderings of Narada Muni mirror the transformative power of storytelling, where every word becomes a portal to fantastical realms, much like the pages of a fantasy book.

As we delve into "The Enchanted Realms: Exploring Fantasy and Creating Worlds," the parallel with Narada

Muni's storytelling odyssey becomes evident-a celebration of the imaginative spark that lights the way to magical lands. This chapter encourages young architects of the fantastical to embrace their storytelling abilities, forging paths into worlds where dragons soar, wizards cast spells, and every word is a brushstroke on the canvas of their boundless imagination. So, inspired by Narada Muni's cosmic tales, let the young dreamweavers embark on their own fantasy odyssey, painting the universe with the hues of their imaginative brilliance.

What is Fantasy?

Imagine a world where wizards cast spells, talking animals share wisdom, and ordinary objects transform into magical artifacts. That, dear dreamers, is the enchanting world of fantasy! Fantasy is the art of weaving tales that transport you to realms beyond reality, where the extraordinary becomes everyday.

1. **Immersive Storytelling:** Close your eyes and imagine a book opening to reveal a world of wizards, fairies, and mythical creatures. Fantasy literature is like a portal that invites you to step into these imaginative lands, where every word is a brushstroke painting the canvas of your mind.

2. **Creatures of Fantasy:** In fantasy, you'll encounter beings straight from the dreams of your imagination. Picture majestic unicorns, mischievous sprites, and fire-breathing dragons. Each creature is a friend waiting to share their story and spark the flames of your creativity.

3. **Magical Places:** Picture castles in the clouds, secret gardens where time stands still, or bustling markets in mystical realms. Fantasy literature takes you on journeys to places that exist only in the pages of books and the corridors of your imagination.

Impact of Fantasy on Imagination

Now, let's uncover the magical influence of fantasy literature on your imagination.

1. **Expanding Horizons:** Fantasy opens doors to new perspectives, allowing you to see the world through the eyes of characters facing impossible challenges. Whether it's overcoming dark sorcery or forging friendships with magical beings, fantasy teaches you to navigate life's adventures with courage and resilience.
2. **Creativity Unleashed:** Fantasy literature is a treasure trove of creativity. It inspires you to think beyond the ordinary, to dream up your creatures, and to imagine worlds where the laws of reality bow to the whims of magic. Your creativity is the magic wand that brings these visions to life.
3. **Building Empathy:** As you journey with characters on their quests, you learn to understand their struggles and triumphs. Fantasy nurtures empathy, teaching you that heroes come in all shapes and sizes, and everyone has a unique story worth telling.
4. **Courage and Hope:** In the face of mythical monsters or daunting quests, characters in fantasy stories often discover newfound courage and hope.

These tales remind you that even in the darkest of times, your inner light can shine brightly, guiding you through challenges.

Encouraging Kids to Create Their Fantasy Worlds

Now, let's set sail on the pirate ship of creativity and chart a course to create your very own fantasy worlds.

1. **Imagination Seeds:**
   - Close your eyes and envision a tiny seed in your hand.
   - Plant this seed in the soil of your imagination.
   - Watch as it grows into a fantastical world with every detail imagined by you.

2. **Character Quest:**
   - Create your fantasy character. What special powers do they have? What's their mission or quest?
   - Draw or write about your character's adventures in a magical land of your own making.

3. **Fantasy Mapmaking:**
   - Grab a sheet of paper and draw a map of your fantasy world.
   - Mark places like the Enchanted Forest, Dragon's Lair, or the Whispering Mountains.
   - Let your imagination guide you as you build your magical geography.

4. Story Stones:

- Collect pebbles or stones from your backyard.
- Paint or draw magical symbols on each stone, creating a set of story stones.
- Toss the stones and let them inspire your next fantastical tale.

☺ Jokes and Quotes Corner ☺

"Fantasy is hardly an escape from reality. It's a way of understanding it."

- Lloyd Alexander

Now, let's add a sprinkle of laughter. **Why did the wizard break up with the broomstick? It wasn't sweeping him off his feet!** *Laughter is the potion that makes your fantasy adventures even more delightful.*

Closing Thoughts: Your Fantasy Odyssey

Dear young adventurers, as you traverse the realms of fantasy, remember the wise words of J.R.R. Tolkien: **"Fantasy is escapist, and that is its glory. If a soldier is imprisoned by the enemy, don't we consider it his duty to escape?"** Your imagination is the key to unlocking worlds beyond the mundane. So, grab your map, unleash your creativity, and let the magic of fantasy guide you on epic journeys. The fantastical realms await your touch - now, go and create your own enchanting tales!

Chapter 8

The Imagination Circus: A Spectacular Show of Creativity

As we step into "The Imagination Circus: A Spectacular Show of Creativity," the tale of Vishwakarma, the divine architect in Hindu mythology, weaves seamlessly into the vibrant fabric of this whimsical chapter. Vishwakarma, the cosmic craftsman, symbolizes the creative and imaginative forces that shape the very essence of our existence.

Much like Vishwakarma's celestial blueprints that intricately design the cosmos, the Imagination Circus becomes an earthly manifestation of divine creativity. The circus tent, a metaphorical canvas, echoes Vishwakarma's celestial workshop, where every act is a spectacle crafted with precision, ingenuity, and an abundance of imagination.

In this grand circus of the mind, young ringmasters and star performers channel the spirit of Vishwakarma, embracing their roles as architects of fantastical ideas. The Imagination Arena mirrors Vishwakarma's divine workshop, offering a space where the delicate balance between reality and the fantastical is explored, much like the tightrope walker navigating the cosmic realms.

So, as the young performers unfold acts of juggling ideas, walking imaginative tightropes, and collaborating like acrobats in a celestial ballet, they embody the spirit of Vishwakarma's creative dance. Let this Imagination Circus be a celebration of divine imagination, where every laugh, wonder, and creative act echoes the cosmic dance of Vishwakarma, guiding the young dreamweavers to create wonders beyond their wildest dreams. The show is ready to begin - now, let the grand spectacle of creativity commence!

The Imagination Circus: Where Creativity Takes Center Stage

Imagine a big, colorful circus tent filled with the buzz of excitement. That's your imagination circus, a place where creativity, joy, and the extraordinary come together in a spectacular show!

1. **The Imagination Arena:** Close your eyes and envision a vast arena under the circus tent. This is your imagination playground, a space where your wildest thoughts become breathtaking acts under the spotlight.

2. **The Creativity Carousel:** Picture a dazzling carousel with vibrant horses representing different ideas and colors. Each spin takes you on a unique ride, exploring new concepts, and discovering the magic within your mind.

3. **The Giggle Circus Tent:** In one corner, imagine a tent dedicated to laughter - the Giggle Circus Tent! Here, jokes, riddles, and whimsical tales unfold, creating an atmosphere where laughter is not just welcome; it's the star of the show.

Creativity on Parade: Acts of Imagination

Now, let's unfold the acts that make the Imagination Circus a must-see spectacle.

1. The Juggler of Ideas:

- Picture a talented juggler tossing ideas high in the air.
- Each idea is a colorful ball, and the juggler skillfully weaves them together.
- Watch as the audience marvels at the seamless flow of creativity.

2. The Tightrope Walker of Imagination:

- Envision a tightrope walker balancing on a thin line high above.
- The tightrope represents the delicate balance between reality and the fantastical.

- Feel the thrill as the walker dances gracefully, inspiring you to explore the edges of your imagination.

3. The Clown of Originality:

- Imagine a playful clown with a suitcase full of surprises.
- The clown's antics bring joy and unexpected twists, encouraging you to embrace the unexpected in your creative endeavors.
- The audience roars with laughter as the clown turns ordinary moments into extraordinary memories.

4. The Acrobats of Collaboration:

- Picture a team of acrobats working together to form intricate human pyramids.
- Each acrobat represents a different skill or idea, showcasing the power of collaboration in creating something greater than the sum of its parts.
- Feel the unity and strength in diversity as the acrobats soar through the air.

😊 Jokes and Quotes Corner 😊

"Creativity is intelligence having fun."

- Albert Einstein.

Now, let's sprinkle in some laughter. **Why don't scientists trust atoms? Because they make up everything!** *Laughter is the secret ingredient that adds a touch of magic to the Imagination Circus. Share your own jokes with friends, and let the joy spread like confetti.*

Interactive Imagination Acts: Join the Circus Fun

1. The Balloon Pop of Ideas:

- Inflate balloons and write different ideas on each one.
- Create a burst of creativity by popping balloons and exploring the ideas inside.
- This lively act encourages you to embrace spontaneity and discover hidden gems within your thoughts.

2. The Magic Hat of Possibilities:

- Imagine a magician's hat filled with slips of paper, each containing a unique scenario or idea.
- Pick a slip, and let your imagination run wild, turning the chosen concept into a vivid mental picture.
- This act inspires you to explore various scenarios and expand your imaginative repertoire.

3. The Storytelling Circus Train:

- Envision a whimsical circus train traveling through your imagination.
- Each train car holds a different story or idea.
- Jump aboard and let your imagination ride the storytelling train to new and exciting destinations.

Closing Grand Finale: Unleashing Your Imagination

Dear young performers of the Imagination Circus, remember the wise words of Pablo Picasso: **"Everything you can imagine is real."** The circus may fold its tents, but your imagination remains a boundless arena of possibilities. So, embrace the creativity, laugh heartily, and let the Imagination Circus be a constant celebration of your extraordinary mind. The show is yours to continue - now, go and create wonders beyond your wildest dreams!

Chapter 9

Art and Expression: Unleashing the Imagination Canvas

As we embark on the enchanting chapter of "Art and Expression: Unleashing the Imagination Canvas," the divine tale of Ganesha's creation by Goddess Parvati seamlessly intertwines with the vibrant strokes of artistic exploration. Ganesha, born from the canvas of Parvati's imagination, becomes a divine testament to the boundless potential of creative thought.

Similar to Parvati shaping Ganesha with the divine touch of imagination, this chapter unfolds as an invitation for young artists to wield their imaginative paintbrushes and sculpt the world of their dreams. The imagination canvas, a metaphorical realm where thoughts bloom into vivid hues, mirrors Parvati's divine act of envisioning and manifesting.

The connection between the divine creation of Ganesha and the artistic expression of young creators becomes evident as the palette of emotions is explored. Every color on the artist's palette echoes the myriad feelings that Parvati breathed into her divine creation. The gallery of dreams, where each artwork is a window into someone's imagination, becomes a homage to Ganesha's unique form born from Parvati's creative brilliance.

So, dear young Picassos and Van Goghs, let this chapter be a celebration of the divine spark within you. As you doodle, sculpt, and create your masterpiece, remember that your artistic expression is a reflection of the divine thought that resides in the heart of creativity. The canvas is yours to explore - now, go and paint the masterpiece that your imagination longs to create!

The Imagination Canvas: Where Dreams Take Shape

Imagine a canvas stretching as far as your eyes can see. This is your imagination canvas, a space where thoughts, feelings, and dreams come alive through the power of artistic expression.

1. **The Brush of Imagination:** Picture a magical paintbrush in your hand. With every stroke, you weave dreams into reality, turning ordinary moments into extraordinary masterpieces. This brush is your imagination's best friend, always ready to bring your inner world to life.

2. **The Palette of Emotions:** Envision a palette filled with a rainbow of emotions. Each color represents a feeling - the warmth of happiness, the coolness of calm, and the vibrant hues of excitement. Your imagination mixes these emotions, creating a symphony of colors that tells your unique story.

3. **The Gallery of Dreams:** Picture an art gallery showcasing the dreams of young artists like yourself. Each painting, sculpture, or creation is a window into someone's imagination. The gallery is a testament to the limitless possibilities of self-expression.

The Connection Between Imagination and Artistic Expression

Now, let's unravel the beautiful threads that connect your imagination to the world of artistic expression.

1. **Imagination Seeds:** Close your eyes and imagine a seed planted in the soil of your mind. This seed is an idea, a spark waiting to bloom. Artistic expression

nurtures these seeds, allowing them to grow into vibrant flowers of creativity.

2. **Stories in Colors:** Imagine a world where every color tells a story. The green of a meadow whispers tales of adventure, while the blue of the sky carries dreams to far-off lands. Through artistic expression, you become a storyteller, painting narratives with your chosen colors.

3. **Shapes of Imagination:** Picture a blank canvas filled with shapes waiting to be brought to life. Whether it's circles dancing in harmony or triangles soaring like birds, your imagination shapes the world around you. Artistic expression is the language that translates these shapes into visual poetry.

4. **Expressing Feelings:** Imagine an emotion bubbling within you, seeking an outlet. Artistic expression provides a canvas for your feelings – joy, sadness, excitement, or curiosity. Through art, you give your emotions a voice, allowing others to understand the colorful symphony within your heart.

Encouraging Kids to Express Themselves Through Art Forms

Now, let's embark on a journey of self-discovery and creative exploration.

1. Doodle Delight:

- Grab a piece of paper and let your hand move freely.

- Doodle whatever comes to mind - shapes, patterns, or even your favorite characters.

- Doodling is a joyful way to express your thoughts without worrying about perfection.

2. Collage Carnival:

- Collect magazines, scissors, and glue.

- Cut out pictures and words that resonate with you.

- Create a collage that reflects your interests, dreams, and the world you imagine.

3. Story Sculpting:

- Use modeling clay, playdough, or any sculpting material.

- Sculpt characters or scenes from a story in your mind.

- Let your hands shape the tale your imagination wants to tell.

4. Poetry Picassos:

- Write a poem expressing your feelings or thoughts.

- Use vivid language and rhythmic patterns to create a visual masterpiece with words.

- Poetry is a unique form of artistic expression that dances with the soul.

😊 Jokes and Quotes Corner 😊

"Every artist was first an amateur."

- Ralph Waldo Emerson.

Now, let's sprinkle in some laughter. **Why did the paintbrush go to therapy? It had too many issues with its strokes!** *Laughter is the paint that adds a splash of joy to your artistic endeavors.*

Closing Masterpiece: Your Imagination Gallery

Dear young Picassos and Van Goghs, remember the wise words of Pablo Picasso: **"Art washes away from the soul the dust of everyday life."** Your artistic expression is a gift to the world, a reflection of your unique perspective. So, paint boldly, sculpt freely, and let your imagination gallery become a testament to the incredible world within you. The canvas is yours to explore - now, go and create your masterpiece!

Chapter 10

The Scientific Imagination: Discovering Wonders through Curiosity

As we delve into the captivating chapter of "The Scientific Imagination: Discovering Wonders through Curiosity," the tale of Dhruva's Meditation seamlessly merges with the spirit of exploration and discovery. Dhruva's profound meditation, driven by unwavering focus and the transformative power of imagination, mirrors the scientific journey where curious minds ignite the spark of innovation.

The Imagination Lab, our metaphorical laboratory of scientific exploration, becomes a nexus where the scientific imagination intertwines with the disciplined focus exhibited by Dhruva. As scientists use their mental Telescope of Possibilities to explore the cosmos, Dhruva's intense meditation becomes a metaphorical microscope, delving into the depths of spiritual realms through focused imagination.

The Question Quest of scientists resonates with Dhruva's inquiry into the divine, aligning with the notion that imagination propels both scientific and spiritual exploration. Dhruva's commitment to reaching the Hypothesis Horizon, seeking the grace of Lord Vishnu, parallels the determination of scientists predicting and navigating the uncharted territories of their experiments.

As we engage in interactive experiments, the synergy between the scientific and spiritual dimensions becomes apparent. Dhruva's Meditation, marked by transformative imagination, offers an insightful parallel to the scientific method, highlighting the interconnectedness of curiosity, focus, and the limitless potential of the human mind.

So, young scientists and explorers, let the scientific imagination be your guide. As you embark on your own Question Quests and Experiment Expeditions, remember the inspiring journey of Dhruva. The laboratory is yours to explore - now, go and uncover the magic of science and the transformative power of focused imagination!

The Imagination Lab: Where Curiosity Takes Flight

Imagine a laboratory filled with bubbling beakers, fizzing potions, and machines that hum with curiosity. Welcome to the Imagination Lab - the place where scientists harness the power of imagination to unlock the mysteries of the universe.

1. **The Inventor's Imagination:** Picture a scientist with wild hair and a twinkle in their eye. This inventor's imagination is a laboratory of its own, where ideas bubble and experiments bloom. The scientific imagination is a force that turns "what if" into "Eureka!"

2. **The Telescope of Possibilities:** Envision a powerful telescope pointed at the stars. This isn't just any telescope; it's the Telescope of Possibilities. Scientists use it to peer into the vast unknown, exploring galaxies, planets, and cosmic wonders with their minds.

3. **The Microscope of Curiosity:** Picture a tiny, magical microscope that reveals the hidden worlds within. Scientists use it to delve into the microscopic realms, discovering the intricate dance of cells, the building blocks of life, and the secrets of the tiniest inhabitants of our planet.

How Scientists Use Imagination in Discovery

Now, let's unravel the secrets of how scientists, like intrepid explorers, navigate the vast landscapes of their imaginations to make ground breaking discoveries.

1. The Question Quest:

- Scientists embark on a quest fueled by curiosity.
- They ask questions like, "Why does the sky change colors?" or "How do plants grow?"
- Your imagination is the compass that guides you on your own question quest.

2. The Experiment Expedition:

- Scientists design experiments to test their ideas.
- Imagine setting up a mini-laboratory in your kitchen or backyard.
- Through experimentation, scientists explore, discover, and refine their understanding of the world.

3. The Hypothesis Horizon:

- Scientists create hypotheses - educated guesses about how things work.
- Imagine predicting what will happen when you mix different ingredients or change variables in an experiment.
- Your imagination is the captain steering your ship toward the horizon of discovery.

4. **The Creative Lab Coat:**
   - Picture scientists donning lab coats adorned with colors, symbols, and patches.
   - These coats aren't just for protection; they're expressions of creativity.
   - Your imagination is your very own creative lab coat, allowing you to approach challenges with flair and innovation.

Fun and Interactive Science Experiments

Now, let's roll up our sleeves and engage in exciting, hands-on experiments that turn your imagination into a laboratory of wonders.

1. **Rainbow in a Jar:**
   - Fill a clear jar with water.
   - Carefully layer different liquids with varying densities, like syrup, dish soap, and oil.
   - Watch as a rainbow forms in the jar, showcasing the magic of density and color mixing.

2. **Balloon Rocket Blast:**
   - Attach a string across a room.
   - Thread a straw onto the string.
   - Blow up a balloon, tape it to the straw, and let go!

- Explore the forces that propel your balloon rocket across the room.

3. Magic Milk Art:
- Pour a shallow layer of milk onto a plate.
- Drop food coloring onto the milk.
- Dip a cotton swab in dish soap and touch the milk.
- Marvel at the swirling colors as the soap interacts with the fat molecules in the milk.

4. DIY Volcano Eruption:
- Create a volcano shape using clay or playdough.
- Place a small cup in the center.
- Mix baking soda and vinegar in the cup for a bubbly eruption.
- Witness the explosive reaction and learn about chemical reactions.

😊 Jokes and Quotes Corner 😊

"Science is magic that works."

- Kurt Vonnegut.

Now, let's add a dash of laughter. **Why did the biologist go on a diet? They wanted to lose some cells!** *Laughter is the catalyst that makes learning even more enjoyable.*

Closing Laboratory Note: Your Scientific Imagination

Dear young scientists, remember the wise words of Marie Curie: **"Nothing in life is to be feared; it is only to be understood."** Your scientific imagination is a beacon that lights the way to understanding the wonders of the universe. So, put on your creative lab coat, pick up your question quest, and let your experiments be the stars in the sky of your imagination. The laboratory is yours to explore - now, go and uncover the magic of science!

Chapter 11

The Mindful Imagination: Where Creativity Meets Presence

As we step into the enchanting chapter of "The Mindful Imagination: Where Creativity Meets Presence," the timeless tale of "The Monkey and the Crocodile" from the Panchatantra seamlessly intertwines with the essence of mindfulness and imaginative exploration. This ancient narrative serves as a parable, illustrating the power of wit and imagination to overcome challenges, a theme that harmoniously resonates with the concept of a Mindful Oasis.

Just as the monkey in the Panchatantra tale navigates the challenges presented by the cunning crocodile through wit and resourcefulness, our journey into mindfulness and imagination becomes a mindful adventure. The Mindful Oasis, depicted as a serene haven, mirrors the strategic focus of the monkey as he traverses the unpredictable waters. In this tranquil oasis, imagination dances with mindfulness, creating a symphony of peace and creativity.

The exercises provided, inspired by both the Monkey and the Crocodile narrative and the principles of mindfulness, aim to enhance focus, spark creativity, and illuminate the path where mindfulness and imagination converge. Just as the monkey utilized his keen awareness and quick thinking, these exercises invite young dreamers to engage their senses mindfully, creating a bridge between the ancient wisdom of fables and the contemporary exploration of mindfulness.

So, young dreamers and mindful adventurers, let "The Monkey and the Crocodile" be your guiding parable. As you breathe life into the Mindful Oasis and embark on imaginative journeys, remember that the magic lies in the union of presence and creativity. The journey is yours to unfold - now, go and explore the wonders of your mindful imagination!

The Mindful Oasis: Where Imagination Blooms

Imagine a serene oasis surrounded by the gentle rustle of leaves, the soothing sounds of a babbling brook, and the fragrance of blooming flowers. This is your Mindful Oasis, a place where imagination and mindfulness dance together, creating a symphony of peace and creativity.

1. **The Breath of Imagination:** Picture your breath as a gentle breeze, moving in and out like the tides. As you breathe, imagine inhaling inspiration and exhaling possibilities. Your breath becomes the rhythm that guides the dance of your imagination.

2. **The Present Palette:** Envision a palette of colors representing each moment. Mindfulness paints the canvas of the present with vibrant hues, allowing you to savor each experience. Your imagination becomes a paintbrush, adding strokes of curiosity to the masterpiece of now.

3. **The Focus Forest:** Picture a forest where each tree symbolizes a moment of focus. Mindfulness helps you navigate this Focus Forest, where the rustling leaves are distractions, and the sturdy trunks represent your centered attention. Your imagination becomes the compass guiding you through the trees.

Connecting Imagination with Mindfulness

Now, let's unravel the thread that connects the boundless realms of your imagination with the peaceful practice of mindfulness.

1. Imagination in the Present Moment:

- Close your eyes and picture a moment from your day.
- Bring your senses into play. What do you see, hear, smell, taste, or feel?

- Imagination and mindfulness collaborate to enrich your experience of the present.

2. Mindful Storytelling:

- Imagine crafting a story in your mind.
- Be mindful of each word, creating a narrative that unfolds with intention.
- Your storytelling becomes a mindful journey where each sentence is a step into the present.

3. Visualizing Mindful Adventures:

- Picture a favorite place or a magical world in your mind.
- Engage your senses to fully immerse yourself in the scene.
- Mindfulness and imagination intertwine, turning visualization into a mindful adventure.

4. Gratitude Garden:

- Imagine a garden where each flower represents something you're grateful for.
- Take a mindful moment to appreciate each petal, color, and fragrance.
- Your gratitude garden becomes a canvas of positive emotions, nurtured by mindfulness and imagination.

Exercises to Enhance Focus and Creativity

Now, let's delve into interactive exercises that will enhance your focus, spark creativity, and illuminate the path where mindfulness and imagination converge.

1. Mindful Breathing Journey:

- Find a comfortable spot and close your eyes.
- Inhale slowly, counting to four. Hold your breath for a moment.
- Exhale slowly, counting to four again.
- As you breathe, imagine your mind boarding a gentle cloud, floating through the sky of tranquility.

2. Sensory Exploration:

- Choose an object, like a seashell or a favorite toy.
- Engage your senses mindfully – feel its texture, notice its colors, and appreciate any sounds it makes.
- Allow your imagination to create a story around the object, turning it into a portal to a different world.

3. Mindful Color Meditation:

- Picture a color in your mind. It could be the soothing blue of the sky or the vibrant green of a meadow.

- As you focus on the color, take slow, mindful breaths.
- Imagine the color spreading through your body, bringing calmness and inspiration.

4. Guided Imagination Walk:

- Take a mindful walk in a safe, quiet space.
- As you walk, let your imagination guide the journey. Picture yourself strolling through a magical forest or along a sparkling beach.
- Engage with the sights, sounds, and sensations, creating a mindful tapestry of your imagination.

☺ Jokes and Quotes Corner ☺

"The present moment is filled with joy and happiness.

If you are attentive, you will see it."

*- **Thich Nhat Hanh.***

Now, let's add a sprinkle of laughter.

Why did the mindful robot go to therapy? It had too many bytes of emotional baggage! *Laughter is the bridge that connects mindfulness and joy.*

Closing Zen Note: Your Mindful Imagination Journey

Dear young explorers, remember the wise words of Lao Tzu: **"When I let go of what I am, I become what I might be."** Your mindful imagination is a journey of self-discovery, a tapestry woven with the threads of presence and creativity. So, let your imagination dance in the embrace of mindfulness, and may your mindful oasis be a sanctuary of joy, focus, and boundless possibilities. The journey continues - now, go and explore the magic within!

Chapter 12

The Problem-Solving Quest: Unleashing Imagination's Superpowers

As we step into the exhilarating chapter of "The Problem-Solving Quest: Unleashing Imagination's Superpowers," the legendary tale of "Hanuman's Leap to Lanka" seamlessly weaves into the fabric of imaginative adventures. This ancient epic serves as a testament to the extraordinary feats attainable through focused intent and imagination, echoing the essence of creative problem-solving explored in this chapter.

Just as Hanuman's leap showcased the boundless potential of physical feats through focused intent, the Adventure Hub becomes a metaphorical stage where young problem solvers harness the power of their imagination to tackle everyday challenges. The imagination backpack, akin to Hanuman's determination, equips these young adventurers with tools crafted from the finest dreams, transforming each problem into an extraordinary quest.

The interactive scenarios and exercises presented draw inspiration from Hanuman's unwavering focus, encouraging young minds to envision solutions, navigate through challenges like a magical maze, invent inventive gadgets in their imagination workshop, and craft creative narratives in the storybook dilemma. Through these scenarios, the chapter bridges the timeless tale with contemporary approaches to problem-solving, inviting young imaginations to soar to new heights.

So, young problem solvers and imaginative adventurers, let **"Hanuman's Leap to Lanka"** be your guiding inspiration. As you embark on the Problem-Solving Quest, remember that the magic lies within your imagination, turning challenges into thrilling adventures. The quest is yours to conquer - now, go and explore the wonders of imaginative problem-solving!

The Adventure Hub: Where Imagination Meets Challenges

Imagine a bustling hub filled with colorful signs pointing in every direction. This is your Adventure Hub, a place where imagination and problem-solving team up to turn ordinary days into extraordinary quests.

1. **The Map of Solutions:** Picture a map unfurling before you, revealing a landscape of challenges. Each problem is a mysterious island waiting to be explored. Your imagination becomes a treasure map, guiding you to discover creative solutions.

2. **The Imagination Backpack:** Envision a magical backpack strapped to your shoulders. Inside, you find tools crafted from the finest dreams - a telescope for foresight, a magnifying glass for attention to detail, and a flashlight to illuminate the darkest problems. Your imagination backpack equips you for any challenge.

3. **The Problem-Solving Compass:** Imagine a compass in your hand, pointing in the direction of imaginative solutions. This compass doesn't rely on north, south, east, or west; it guides you toward possibilities, creativity, and the wonders of problem-solving adventures.

Using Imagination to Solve Everyday Problems

Now, let's unravel the secrets of how imagination transforms into a superhero when it comes to solving everyday problems.

1. Imagination as a Detective:

- Imagine you're a detective solving a mystery.
- Analyze the clues - what's causing the problem?

- Your imagination helps you see the bigger picture and connect the dots.

2. The Superpower of "What If?":
- Close your eyes and ask, "What if?"
- Imagine different scenarios where the problem doesn't exist or where solutions magically appear.
- Your "What If" superpower sparks creative thinking and opens new pathways.

3. The Time-Traveling Imagination:
- Picture a time machine in your mind.
- Travel forward and backward in time to explore how the problem evolves.
- Your imagination time-travels to unveil insights and potential solutions.

4. Creative Collaboration:
- Imagine gathering a team of imaginary friends or superheroes.
- Each friend contributes unique ideas and perspectives.
- Your imagination turns problem-solving into a collaborative adventure.

Interactive Problem-Solving Scenarios

Now, let's embark on interactive scenarios that will transform you into a problem-solving maestro.

1. **The Magical Maze Mystery:**
   - Imagine you're in a maze filled with challenges.
   - Each turn presents a problem - how will you navigate?
   - Use your imagination to visualize solutions and navigate through the magical maze.

2. **The Inventor's Workshop:**
   - Picture a workshop filled with gadgets and gizmos.
   - Choose a problem and invent a magical device to solve it.
   - Your imagination turns you into an inventor, crafting solutions with creativity.

3. **The Storybook Dilemma:**
   - Imagine you're a character in a story facing a problem.
   - Write or draw how your character creatively solves the problem.

- Your imagination transforms storytelling into a problem-solving adventure.

4. The Dreamy Detective Agency:
- Envision a detective agency in your mind.
- Take on a case (problem) and gather clues using your imagination.
- Your imagination detective skills lead you to ingenious solutions.

☺ Jokes and Quotes Corner ☺

"Imagination is more important than knowledge."

- Albert Einstein.

Now, let's add a touch of laughter. **Why did the computer go to Doctor? It has viral Infection!** *Laughter is the magic wand that turns problems into puzzles waiting to be solved.*

Closing Adventure Note: Your Problem-Solving Imagination

Dear young adventurers, remember the wise words of Walt Disney: **"It's kind of fun to do the impossible."** Your imagination is the key that unlocks the door to possibilities, turning problems into exciting challenges. So, don your imagination backpack, grab your problem-solving compass, and let each challenge become a new chapter in your problem-solving adventure. The quest is yours to conquer - now, go and explore the wonders of imaginative problem-solving!

Chapter 13

The Collaborative Imagination Carnival: A Celebration of Shared Creativity

As we step into the enchanting chapter of "The Collaborative Imagination Carnival," the ancient tale of "The Churning of the Ocean (Samudra Manthan)" emerges as a profound illustration of the extraordinary results born from collaborative imagination. In this mythological narrative, Devas and Asuras join forces, churning the ocean to obtain the elixir of immortality, showcasing the inherent power when diverse minds unite toward a common goal.

The Collaborative Imagination Carnival becomes a modern-day manifestation of this celestial churning, where imaginative minds converge in a vibrant celebration of shared creativity. The Friendship Ferris Wheel, Carousel of Collaboration, and Funhouse of Ideas become metaphors for the dynamic synergy that arises when individuals contribute their unique ideas, perspectives, and talents to the collaborative canvas.

The group activities and interactive scenarios within the carnival draw inspiration from the mythological collaboration, fostering a sense of unity and shared purpose. Storytelling relays, imagination Pictionary, and group doodle fusion mirror the collaborative spirit of Devas and Asuras, illustrating how collective strokes of imagination create masterpieces beyond individual capabilities.

So, young dreamweavers and collaborative creators, let "The Churning of the Ocean" be your guiding inspiration. As you step into the Collaborative Imagination Carnival, remember that the magic lies in the unity of your creative minds. Embrace the joyous motion of the Friendship Ferris Wheel, let the carousel of collaboration spin with collective ideas, and allow the Funhouse of Ideas to reflect the kaleidoscope of your imaginative diversity. The carnival is yours to lead - now, go and create wonders together!

The Imagination Carnival: Where Dreams Join Hands

Imagine a lively carnival with colorful tents, laughter echoing in the air, and a spirit of collaboration buzzing around. This is your Imagination Carnival, a place where the joy of shared creativity transforms ordinary moments into extraordinary adventures.

1. **The Friendship Ferris Wheel:** Picture a grand Ferris wheel with seats for every friend and collaborator. As it turns, each seat represents a unique idea, perspective, or talent. Your imagination becomes the engine that keeps the Friendship Ferris Wheel spinning.

2. **The Carousel of Collaboration:** Envision a carousel adorned with whimsical animals and characters. Each collaboration is a magical ride, where everyone contributes to the joyous motion. Your imagination becomes the music that sets the carousel in motion.

3. **The Funhouse of Ideas:** Imagine a funhouse filled with mirrors that reflect creative thoughts in every direction. Each mirror represents a different viewpoint, inspiring a kaleidoscope of ideas. Your imagination becomes the guide through the twists and turns of the Funhouse of Ideas.

Group Activities that Foster Shared Imagination

Now, let's unfold the curtain on group activities that transform collaboration into a magical journey of shared imagination.

1. **Storytelling Relay:**
   - Gather a group of friends or classmates.
   - Start a story with a single sentence, then let each person add a sentence to build the narrative.
   - Watch as your collective imagination weaves a unique and unpredictable tale.

2. **Imagination Pictionary:**
   - Create a large canvas or use a whiteboard.
   - Choose a theme (like outer space, underwater, or a fantasy world).
   - Each person takes turns drawing a part of the imaginative scene.
   - Witness how your collaborative strokes create a masterpiece of shared imagination.

3. **Group Doodle Fusion:**
   - Provide a large piece of paper and markers.
   - Begin a doodle or drawing, then pass it to the next person to add their creative touch.
   - Keep passing the paper until everyone has contributed to the collaborative doodle.

4. **Invention Workshop:**
   - Imagine you're in an invention workshop with your friends.
   - Each person suggests an element of a fantastical invention (e.g., wings, teleportation).
   - Collaboratively sketch or describe how this imaginative invention would work.

Encouraging Teamwork and Creativity

Now, let's explore ways to foster teamwork and creativity within your collaborative carnival.

1. **Carnival of Compliments:**
   - Create a circle with your friends or group.
   - Each person takes a turn complimenting the person on their right.
   - Encourage kind and imaginative compliments, celebrating each other's unique qualities.

2. **Imagination Building Blocks:**
   - Provide building blocks or crafting materials.
   - In pairs or small groups, collaboratively build something imaginative.
   - The key is to work together, combining ideas and perspectives to create a cohesive structure.

3. Team Treasure Hunt:

- Organize a treasure hunt with clues that require collaboration.
- Each clue reveals a part of the story, and only by working together can the group reach the final treasure.
- Encourage communication, problem-solving, and imaginative thinking.

😊 Jokes and Quotes Corner 😊

"Alone, we can do so little; together,

we can do so much."

- Helen Keller

Now, let's add a dash of laughter. ***Why did the banana go to the party with the orange? Because it wanted to have a-peeling company!*** *Laughter is the glue that binds collaborative spirits.*

Closing Circus Note: Your Collaborative Imagination Spectacle

Dear young ringmasters and collaborative performers, remember the wise words of Margaret Mead: **"Never doubt that a small group of thoughtful, committed citizens can change the world. Indeed, it's the only thing that ever has."** Your collaborative imagination is a spectacle that transforms shared dreams into reality.

So, gather your friends, embrace the carousel of ideas, and let your collaborative carnival become a celebration of creativity. The show is yours to lead - now, go and create wonders together!

Chapter 14

---※---

Imagination Across Borders

Greetings, young cultural explorers, as we prepare to embark on a global odyssey in "Imagination Across Borders." Before we set sail, let's draw inspiration from "The Yaksha Prashna" in the Mahabharata. Yudhishthira's profound answers to the questions posed by a Yaksha highlight the transformative power of wisdom, intellect, and imagination.

Similarly, our journey into diverse cultures is a quest for understanding, where imagination becomes the key to unlocking the treasures of global creativity. Picture the Yaksha as a symbol of the diverse cultural narratives we are about to encounter-each question an invitation to explore, learn, and appreciate the richness of imagination across borders.

In "Imagination Across Borders," our Cultural Kaleidoscope unfolds to reveal the Dance of Diversity, the Language of Legends, and the Feast of Festivals. We traverse continents, embracing the artistry of Japanese Haiku, the warmth of African Oral Storytelling, the vibrancy of Indian Rangoli, and the mysticism of Mayan Dreamweaving.

Transforming this journey into a creative classroom, we learn not only from textbooks but from the living cultures that shape our world. The global story circle we create becomes a testament to the universal language of imagination, fostering connections across languages and borders.

As we navigate this expedition, remember the profound words of Augustine of Hippo: "The world is a book, and those who do not travel read only one page." With laughter as our universal companion, let's open our Cultural Kaleidoscope, cherish the wisdom of diverse cultures, and paint the canvas of our imagination with the colors of unity. Now, young explorers, let the global adventure begin!

The Cultural Kaleidoscope: Where Imagination Knows No Boundaries

Imagine standing in front of a colossal kaleidoscope, turning it slowly to reveal a myriad of colors, patterns, and stories. This is your Cultural Kaleidoscope, a place where imagination blossoms in countless ways, reflecting the unique creativity of cultures around the world.

1. **The Dance of Diversity:** Picture a global dance where each culture contributes its unique steps. The Dance of Diversity celebrates the richness of imagination, with each culture bringing its own rhythm, melody, and flair to the grand stage.

2. **The Language of Legends:** Envision a library filled with books from every corner of the world. Each book is a treasure trove of cultural legends, myths, and stories. The Language of Legends speaks to the power of imagination in preserving and sharing cultural heritage.

3. **The Feast of Festivals:** Imagine a grand feast with tables adorned with dishes from diverse cuisines. The Feast of Festivals is a celebration where the aroma of creativity wafts through the air, showcasing how imagination is expressed in culinary traditions.

Imagination in Different Cultures: A Global Odyssey

Now, let's set sail on a global odyssey to explore how imagination takes shape in different cultures.

1. Japanese Haiku Harmony:

- Imagine the serenity of a Japanese garden.

- Haiku, a traditional form of poetry, captures fleeting moments with vivid images.

- Your imagination embraces simplicity, harmony, and the beauty of nature through the art of haiku.

2. African Oral Storytelling:

- Picture a circle of people gathered around a fire.
- In many African cultures, storytelling is an oral tradition passed down through generations.
- Your imagination weaves tales of wisdom, bravery, and the interconnectedness of life.

3. Indian Rangoli Radiance:

- Envision colorful patterns adorning the entrance of a home during a festival.
- Rangoli is an Indian art form that uses vibrant powders or flower petals to create intricate designs.
- Your imagination dances with colors, expressing joy, prosperity, and creativity.

4. Mayan Dreamweaving Wisdom:

- Imagine standing before an ancient Mayan temple.
- Mayan culture values dreamweaving, the belief that dreams are messages from the gods.

- Your imagination explores the mystical realm of dreams, seeking wisdom and inspiration.

Learning from Diverse Perspectives: A Creative Classroom

Now, let's transform our global exploration into a creative classroom where we learn valuable lessons from diverse perspectives.

1. **Cultural Art Exchange:**
   - Choose an art form or craft from a different culture.
   - Create your own artwork inspired by that cultural expression.
   - Your imagination becomes a bridge, connecting you to the creative spirit of another community.

2. **Language Treasure Hunt:**
   - Learn a few words or phrases from languages spoken in different countries.
   - Organize a language treasure hunt, where you match words to their respective cultures.
   - Your imagination becomes a linguistic explorer, embracing the beauty of diverse languages.

3. Global Story Circle:

- Invite friends or classmates to share stories from their cultural backgrounds.
- Create a global story circle where each person contributes a tale.
- Your imagination becomes a storyteller, connecting cultures through the universal language of narrative.

☺Jokes and Quotes Corner☺

"The world is a book, and those who do not travel read only one page."

- Augustine of Hippo

Now, let's add a sprinkle of laughter. **Why did the globe go to therapy? It had too many issues with its world view!** *Laughter is the universal language that brings joy across continents.*

Closing Passport Note: Your Global Imagination Expedition

Dear young globetrotters and cultural dreamers, remember the wise words of Nelson Mandela: **"If you talk to a man in a language he understands, that goes to his head. If you talk to him in his language, that goes to his heart."** Your global imagination expedition is a passport to understanding, empathy, and a celebration of diversity. So, open your Cultural

Kaleidoscope, cherish the lessons from different cultures, and let your imagination soar beyond borders. The world is your canvas - now, go and paint it with the colors of unity and creativity!

Chapter 15

---※---

Reflection and Celebration Carnival

Greetings, young dream architects and celebration enthusiasts! As we step into the grand finale, "Reflection and Celebration Carnival," let us draw inspiration from the joyous return of Lord Rama to Ayodhya after vanquishing the formidable Ravana. Rama's triumphant homecoming was a jubilation of bravery, resilience, and the ultimate victory of righteousness.

In our imaginative journey, the Carnival of Reflection unfolds like a fairground adorned with mirrors of diverse shapes and sizes. Each mirror reflects a distinct stage of our imaginative odyssey, mirroring the first spark of an idea, the elation of creation, and the conquest of challenges. Much like Rama's journey, we celebrate the moments that enriched our imaginative world.

The Mirror of Moments captures the essence of our journey, showcasing the initial sparks and triumphs. The Mirror of Challenges reflects our encounters with obstacles, transforming them into stepping stones of resilience. The Mirror of Friendship gleams with the shared creativity and laughter echoing through imaginative collaborations, much like the camaraderie found in Rama's loyal companions.

As we shift our focus to individual creativity, the Imagination Show and Tell, Dream Journal Journey, and Creative Collage Chronicle become showcases of personal brilliance, mirroring Rama's return with each architect showcasing their unique contributions.

Celebrating collective creativity, the Collaborative Showcase, Global Imagination Gallery, and Imagination Appreciation Circle echo the jubilation that marked Rama's return to Ayodhya. Our collective brilliance shines through, reminiscent of the festivities that lit up the city after Rama's victorious homecoming.

In the spirit of this festive celebration and the words of Lord Rama's epic tale, let the Carnival of Reflection be a joyful pause, where we celebrate the individual and collective wonders discovered in our imaginative journey. Walk through the mirrors, showcase your treasures, and let the echoes of celebration linger. The carnival is yours to embrace - now, young celebrants, revel in the carnival of your own creativity!

The Carnival of Reflection: Mirrors of Imagination

Imagine strolling through a carnival adorned with mirrors of all shapes and sizes. Each mirror reflects a different stage of your imagination journey. Welcome to the Carnival of Reflection, where we pause to gaze into the mirrors and appreciate the growth, inspiration, and dreams that have shaped us.

1. **Mirror of Moments:** Picture a mirror reflecting moments from your imagination journey - the first spark of an idea, the joy of creation, and the overcoming of challenges. This mirror invites you to cherish the unique moments that have enriched your imaginative world.

2. **Mirror of Challenges:** Envision a mirror that reflects the challenges you've encountered. Yet, in this mirror, challenges are transformed into stepping stones of resilience and determination. It shows the strength of your imagination in navigating obstacles and turning them into opportunities.

3. **Mirror of Friendship:** Picture a mirror showcasing the friends and collaborators you've met along the way. This mirror celebrates the beauty of shared creativity, the laughter echoing in collaborative endeavors, and the strength found in the tapestry of imaginative friendships.

Celebrating Individual Creativity: A Creative Showcase

Now, let's turn our attention to celebrating the unique creativity that resides within each young imagination architect.

1. **Imagination Show and Tell:**

   - Choose a creation that represents a memorable part of your imagination journey.
   - Share it with friends, family, or a group, explaining the inspiration and process behind it.
   - Your creation becomes a star in the Imagination Show and Tell, a showcase of individual brilliance.

2. **Dream Journal Journey:**

   - Look back through your dream journal or a collection of imaginative ideas.
   - Pick a favorite dream or idea and expand on it, adding new details or twists.
   - Your dream journal becomes a treasure chest, housing the evolving wonders of your imagination.

3. **Creative Collage Chronicle:**

   - Collect images, words, or symbols that represent your imaginative adventures.

- Create a collage that tells the story of your creative journey.
- Your creative collage becomes a visual diary, capturing the essence of your imaginative explorations.

Celebrating Collective Creativity: A Tapestry of Joy

Now, let's celebrate the collective creativity that emerges when imaginative minds join forces.

1. Collaborative Showcase:

- Gather creations from collaborative projects or activities.
- Host a showcase where each contributor presents their role and the imaginative spark they brought to the collaboration.
- Your collaborative showcase becomes a gallery of shared creativity, reflecting the beauty of teamwork.

2. Global Imagination Gallery:

- Display creations inspired by different cultures or perspectives explored in previous chapters.
- Invite others to view the gallery and share their thoughts on the diverse expressions of imagination.

- Your global imagination gallery becomes a testament to the richness of creative diversity.

3. Imagination Appreciation Circle:

- Form a circle with friends or a group.
- Take turns expressing appreciation for each other's imaginative contributions.
- Your imagination appreciation circle becomes a joyful reminder of the collective brilliance within your creative community.

😊Jokes and Quotes Corner😊

"Creativity is intelligence having fun."

- Albert Einstein

Now, let's add a sprinkle of laughter. **Why did the pencil go to the party alone? It wanted to draw attention!** *Laughter is the confetti that makes celebrations even more delightful.*

Closing Celebration Note: Your Imagination Festival

Dear young celebrants and imaginative pioneers, remember the wise words of Dr. Seuss: **"Think and wonder, wonder and think."** Your imagination journey is a festival of wonders and thoughts, a celebration of the unique and collective creativity that makes each step memorable. So, walk through the Carnival of Reflection mirrors, showcase your imaginative treasures, and let the joyous echoes of celebration linger in the air. The festival is yours to embrace - now, go and dance in the carnival of your own creativity!

।। यं यं चिन्तयते कामं तं तं प्राप्नोति निश्चितम् ।।

In the tale of life, where wisdom is spun,
A journey begins for each and every one.

In pages divine, a story unfolds,
Where human perfection and thought are entwined,
we're told.

Let these words be a guide, a spark so bright,
Igniting your quest for knowledge, pure and light.

As an author of dreams, I wish you the best,
On this intellectual odyssey, embark on this quest.

Explore the realms written, with curiosity keen,
Unlock the potential, let your mind intervene.

A gift of introspection, to yourself be kind,
Navigate wisdom's corridors, the treasures you'll find.

In the pages, sculpt your path, young mind,
Towards mastery and wisdom, let your dreams bind.

For in the world of words, you shall discover,
The magic of learning, a journey like no other.

Madhur & Rakesh

www.ingramcontent.com/pod-product-compliance
Lightning Source LLC
LaVergne TN
LVHW061553070526
838199LV00077B/7033